Introduction

Do you remember the darkest day of your life? That day is unlike any other day. For some, the darkest day is much longer than 24 hours. That difficult day could last one year, or ten years. This is because the darkest day of your life often initiates a succession of unforeseen issues that you never had to deal with before.

In this book, you will see how God in His mercy and faithfulness will take the darkest day of your life and use it for destiny. If you are struggling in the aftermath of "what once was," this book will give you the hope that God's Word has promised: "There is hope in thine end" (Jeremiah 31:1).

You will also receive a "blueprint for blessing" through reading this book. You will learn the supernatural steps of how to come back after a crisis, and you will see that God truly is the Rebuilder of Your Ruins.

This book is designed with your destiny in mind. My intent is to show you that all of the promises that God gave to Zion, He also gives to you. These are promises of consolation in the midst of desolation. After Zion was plundered by the Babylonians, she lay desolate and forsaken without walls, without hope, without inhabitants, without dream, and without destiny. But God promised Zion that she would dream again, and so will you: "When the Lord turned the captivity of Zion, we were like them that dream" (Psalm 126:1).

God promised Zion that she would be rebuilt, and that the "children of the desolate would be more than the married wife" (Isaiah 54:1). God also promised Zion that her name would be changed: "You shall be named a new name which the mouth of the Lord shall name" (Isaiah 62:2). This means a change and a new identity. It means reconstruction after the destruction.

Through reading this book, you will also understand and receive the promises of how God will reward your tribulation with divine compensation. This is a promise revealed not only in Isaiah 61:7, but is also one of the most important principles of Jeremiah's prophecies to Zion. It is the promise that God gives to Rachel in Jeremiah 31:37 concerning her tears: "Refrain thy voice from weeping and thine eyes from tears: for thy work shall be rewarded."

Beloved, I believe this is going to be the best season of your life. I believe God is going to rebuild every area of your life. I cannot wait to see what God is going to do with you.

Sincerely,

Dr. Michelle Corral +

Chapter One

Mourning Into Miracles

Have you ever said, "When will I get my life back? When will it ever stop hurting? What does it mean to experience restoration after devastation?" In a literal sense, ruins are the aftermath of a devastating experience. We have all experienced losses on various levels in our lives that we can refer to as "ruins." Some losses are more devastating and excruciating than others. The English word ruin is taken from the Latin word *ruina*, which means "to collapse." For some of us, our ruins can be a collapse in our career or the loss of a loved one. For others, it can be the blatant reality of what never existed. And for some of us, our ruins can be the memory of a broken marriage, certain traumas in our childhood, or disappointed dreams. Every single one of us can relate to the pain of grieving over a loss that we can call our ruins.

When there is physical pain, usually an MRI or an X-ray can detect the position where damage has occurred. Emotional

MC+

We serve a God whose redeeming power turns our devastation into restoration.

pain, however, can be much more challenging to detect. An "emotional MRI" does not exist that can detect such damage. But there is hope for everyone who has experienced loss on any level. We serve a God whose redeeming power turns our devastation into restoration.

Beloved, in this chapter we will see how the Lord promises restoration out of the ruins of our lives. God has given His guarantee that He will bring supernatural reconstruction after the destruction of our devastated dreams. Let's take a look at God's promises to us in the book of Zechariah.

Zechariah 8:18-19 KJV
[18] And the word of the Lord of hosts came unto me, saying, [19] Thus saith the Lord of hosts; The fast of the fourth month, and the fast of the fifth, and the fast of the seventh, and the fast of the tenth, shall be to the house of Judah joy and gladness, and cheerful feasts; therefore love the truth and peace.

To give us some background, the four fasts mentioned here refer to painful times in Israel's history. During different periods of time centuries apart, the Holy Temple in Jerusalem has been destroyed; the First Temple was destroyed by the Babylonians, and the Second Temple was annihilated by the Romans. The fast of the fourth month (of the Biblical calendar) refers to the breaking down of the walls of Jerusalem by the Babylonians, and the fast of the fifth month refers to the destruction of the Temple. The fast of the seventh month refers to the assassination of Gedaliah, a Jewish leader who had been appointed to govern Jerusalem after the First Temple had been destroyed and the city burned, and the fast of the tenth month refers to the time that the Babylonians began to besiege Jerusalem.

While each of these four fast days indicates a sorrowful time in Israel's history, the 21 day period between the fast of the fourth month of the Biblical calendar (seventeenth day of Tammuz) and the fast of the fifth month (ninth day of Av) represents a particularly painful period for the Jewish people. On the seventeenth day of Tammuz, after the children of Israel had left Egypt, Moses came down after 40 days on Mount Sinai, and found many of the Israelites worshiping the golden calf. Centuries later, we see that the seventeenth of Tammuz is also the day that the walls of both the First and Second Temples were breached by attacks from the enemy. Then on the eighth day of Av, back in the time of Moses, we see that 10 of the 12 spies returned with an evil report about the land of Canaan. That night, on the ninth of Av, the people began to cry out and said that they would rather go back to Egypt, which greatly displeased the Lord, and the Jews of that generation were forbidden to enter the Promised Land. Centuries later, the ninth of Av was also the day that the First Temple was completely destroyed by the Babylonians and the Second Temple by the Romans. The ninth day of Av is also called Tisha B'Av, and represents a day of great destruction and devastation.

So we understand that this 21-day period from the seventeenth day of Tammuz to the ninth day of Av has long been a time of mourning and weeping for the Jewish people. It's almost impossible for us to comprehend the mourning and weeping of the children of Israel for the city of Zion, the great city of God, the apple of God's eye. Zion is the greatest treasure in all the earth to the Lord. Zion was founded by King David, and is the city of the Great King. When David became king, one of the first things that he did was establish a city where God would be King. He conquered the city of Jebus, which had been a stronghold of the Jebusites, and captured it for the Lord; this became the city of Zion, or Jerusalem. This was a *Kiddush Hashem*, an act which blessed the Lord and sanctified His name, because the Jebusites had long been in the Promised Land; even Joshua had not been able to drive them out of the Land. But David was determined to lift up God's name and establish the city of Zion for God, to set up His throne in the city and build a tabernacle for the Ark of the Covenant. David's desire was to get the Ark out of obscurity and enthrone it in the city of Jerusalem that he had founded.

When the Ark was finally brought back to Zion from Kirjathjearim, where it had remained during the reign of Saul, David and the children of Israel hallowed the presence of God as they brought the Ark back to Jerusalem; they gave burnt offerings and peace offerings to the Lord every six paces, praising and worshiping the Lord (see 2 Samuel 6).

So David established Zion as the city of the great King. This is why Zion is so precious to God. There is no other place on earth that is as dear to the heart of God as Zion. Zion and Jerusalem are synonymous terms. The name "Zion" is used because it was on the mount of Zion that the Temple was built and the Ark was eventually enthroned; the Tabernacle of David was also placed on Mount Zion and housed the Ark before the Temple was built. During the period of Rehoboam, King David's grandson, Israel split into two kingdoms. The northern kingdom was called Israel with its capital in Samaria, and the southern kingdom was called Judah with its capital in Jerusalem, or Zion. The 10 northern tribes were scattered to the ends of the earth during the Assyrian captivity, but Judah miraculously escaped exile and destruction until it too became so corrupt that God's glory lifted off the city and returned to heaven (Ezekiel 1:1-28).

Dr. Michelle Corral

Ezekiel 11:23a KJV
And the glory of the LORD went up from the midst of the city.

The city became an open target for the enemy without the glory of God. In the holy city of Zion, God's treasure on earth, was found lying, cheating, slander, baseless hatred, robbery, adultery, and idolatry as a way of life.

God's heart was breaking for Zion. So great was His love for the holy city that all of the "latter prophets" (*nevi'im acharonim*) including Isaiah, Jeremiah, Ezekiel, and the prophets of the Trei Azar (the minor prophets), were called to warn Zion, except for Amos and Hosea, who were called to the northern kingdom. These prophets warned Zion of the coming devastation, but more importantly they promised Messianic restoration. All of the prophets that were sent prophesied the rebuilding of the ruins. They prophesied consolation in the places of desolation. In the book of the Isaiah, the final 27 chapters are dedicated to the promises of divine compensation, consolation, and restoration of the ruins. I call these the "Messianic Miracles of Devastation Turned into Restoration."

During the time of Nebuchadnezzar, the walls of Zion began to be barraged on the seventeenth day of Tammuz (fourth Biblical month), and were completely annihilated 21 days later by the ninth day of Av (fifth Biblical month). These 21 days were days of destruction, desolation, and fire, of being taken captive and taken to Babylon. But God prophesied through Zechariah that these grievous months that were months of mourning would become a time of miracles.

Beloved, the words of comfort that the Almighty gave to Zion, He gives to you concerning your devastated dreams and lost hope. The 21 days that were formerly days of destruction beginning with the breaching of the walls are now days of reconstruction and rebuilding because of the Messiah. In every place of ruin and devastation, He is promising your restoration.

It is God's will to turn the darkest days of your life and use them for destiny. Have you ever asked yourself, "Why should I hope again? I just can't handle another disappointment." Some of us have been through so many periods of pain in our lives that we cannot bear the anxiety of another shattered dream.

MC+
It is God's will to turn the darkest days of your life and use them for destiny.

Beloved, let me share with you about the promises that God has given to Zion, the city that became ransacked and in ruins. These are promises given to those who mourn for Zion. The days of mourning for Zion because of the destruction of the two Temples (several hundred years apart on the same day) are called the 21-day mourning period. They are 21 days of mourning for the ashes, the ruins, and the destruction of Solomon's Temple, the rebuilt Temple, and the city of Jerusalem that was sacked by the Babylonians and later the Romans.

MC+

God has promised in His Word that the weeping will be turned to reaping.

The 21 days of mourning for Zion are observed by national fasts. God has promised in His Word that the weeping will be turned to reaping. He has promised that the days of mourning will become days of miracles. God has promised that the 21 days that were designated to mourn for the devastation shall now become days of restoration. Let's look again at the promises that God has spoken concerning the consolation after the devastation.

Zechariah 8:18-19 KJV
[18] And the word of the Lord of hosts came unto me, saying, [19] Thus saith the Lord of hosts; The fast of the fourth month, and the fast of the fifth, and the fast of the seventh, and the fast of the tenth, shall be to the house of Judah joy and gladness, and cheerful feasts; therefore love the truth and peace.

God was saying that no matter what Zion had been through, and no matter what each one of us has been through, He is promising restoration after the ruin. No matter what the crisis, God promises a comeback. We may have experienced a divorce, death in the family, loss of a home or a career, loss of income, or loss of reputation, but there will be restoration after the ruin.

God wants to heal the areas which have caused us to cry the most, the areas connected with our deepest, most painful tears. Tears can express the feelings of the soul. We can speak with our mouths and express the feelings of our rational minds, but there are some things that can't be communicated through our voices. Tears are a way to communicate what our souls are experiencing. Sometimes when tears come forth in excessive weeping, it is a type of travail in our soul that indicates that we know that this is not the end of the story, that God has something more for us.

Jeremiah 31:15-16 KJV
[15] Thus saith the Lord; A voice was heard in Ramah, lamentation, and bitter weeping; Rachel weeping for her children refused to be comforted for her children, because they were not. [16] Thus saith the Lord; Refrain thy voice from weeping, and thine eyes from tears: for thy work shall be rewarded, saith the Lord; and they shall come again from the land of the enemy.

Dr. Michelle Corral

MC+

God wants us to experience the deepest inner healing of our lives.

During this season, God wants us to experience the deepest inner healing of our lives. The places of our soul that have been mute, that have unexpressed pain, that have been shoved down and stuffed, all the emotional hurts – this is the time that God wants us to express the pain in our souls because this is the time of our deliverance.

Beloved, we need to understand that every word that God gave to Zion, He also gave to the church through the Messiah. Israel is God's firstborn, His chosen. We do not replace Israel, but the Messiah has made us partakers of the promises that God gave to Israel (Ephesians 2:11-13). Nothing can take the place of literal Zion, but we need to see what John the beloved disciple said in the book of Revelation.

Revelation 21:2 KJV
And I John saw the holy city, new Jerusalem, coming down from God out of heaven, prepared as a bride adorned for her husband.

We need to realize that the new Zion is the church, and as much as God loves literal Zion, He also loves the church, because the church is likened unto Zion. That means that

Dr. Michelle Corral

every promise that God gave to Zion, God is giving to each one of us.

We also need to understand that the movement called *Shivat Zion*, or the return to Zion, began under the prophet Ezra. When Ezra began to lead the Israelites from Babylon back to Zion, this was a fulfillment of Jeremiah's prophecy. These texts promise the repossession of taken territory. This means that you will repossess every promise that God has given you concerning your destiny. He will perform every promise concerning bringing you back. Nothing can drive you out of your destiny.

MC+
You will repossess every promise that God has given you concerning your destiny.

Jeremiah 29:10 KJV
For thus saith the Lord, That after seventy years be accomplished at Babylon I will visit you, and perform my good word toward you, in causing you to return to this place.

You may feel distanced away from your destiny, but the Lord has promised that just like He remembered the children of Israel and brought them out of the land of darkness back into the land of promise, He will do the same for us. God has been preparing us for a shift in our season. Let's take a look at Psalm 102.

Psalm 102:13 KJV
Thou shalt arise, and have mercy upon Zion: for the time to favour her, yea, the set time, is come.

Promises of Shivat Zion for You

Promise 1: *Your Mourning Will Be Turned to Miracles*

The first promise of Shivat Zion is that our time of mourning will be transformed into a time of great miracles. You may be thinking, "I haven't been able to dream because I've been so caught up in trying to survive that I've surrendered my dreams. But during this time of Shivat Zion, my dreams are coming back. I am dreaming about taking back territory, rebuilding, and expansion. I am dreaming about how God is going to be faithful to everything that He has promised me!" Beloved, we can see God's promises in Psalm 126 concerning Shivat Zion and the restoration of ruin in our lives.

Psalm 126:1 KJV
When the Lord turned again the captivity of Zion, we were like them that dream.

Dr. Michelle Corral

Psalm 126:2 KJV
Then was our mouth filled with laughter, and our tongue with singing: then said they among the heathen, The Lord hath done great things for them.

The changes that took place in the lives of the Israelites were so dramatic that the heathen noticed and said that this was the hand of the Lord: as we see in the last half of Psalm 126:2 above, "Then said they among the heathen, The Lord hath done great things for them." When the Lord brought Israel out of captivity, the heathen that used to mock the children of Israel declared these great things were being done by God Himself. Similarly, God is going to bring each of us out of captivity and fill our mouths with laughter. This is not the time to sit back and sulk and get into depression – no! God has promised that everything about our countenance will become laughter and joy and singing. We will live in days of God's blessing and goodness. This divine shift in our circumstances is a Messianic miracle!

MC+
God has promised that everything about our countenance will become laughter and joy and singing.

Promise 2: *The Cancellation of Your Captivity*

The second promise of Shivat Zion that we see in Psalm 126 is that God is going to cancel our captivity. God is going to bring us out of a painful place into a land of promise.

Psalm 126:4 KJV
Turn again our captivity, O Lord, as the streams in the south.

In other words, the streams were flowing back to Zion. This meant that hundreds and hundreds of captives were coming back to Zion, singing on their way because the captivity had been cancelled. For this season, the warfare had been accomplished. Praise the Lord for cancelling the captivity in our lives!

Promise 3: *Supernatural Reaping in the Places You Are Weeping*

The third promise of Shivat Zion that we see in Psalm 126 is that we will experience supernatural reaping in every place of our weeping.

Psalm 126:5-6 KJV
[5] They that sow in tears shall reap in joy. [6] He that goeth forth and weepeth, bearing precious seed, shall

doubtless come again with rejoicing, bringing his sheaves with him.

Promise 4: *God Will Reverse Your Shame and Restore Your Name*

God also promises to reverse our shame and restore our name. Therapists describe shame as a mindset of believing that others devalue us and don't think highly of us. In the days of Ezra and Nehemiah, Zion had become a place of mockery and shame; the nations of the world mocked God and the Jews. According to Nehemiah 4:2, Sanballat scorned the children of Israel, saying, "What do these feeble Jews? Will they fortify themselves? Will they sacrifice? Will they make an end in a day? Will they revive the stones out of the heaps of the rubbish which are burned?" The Israelites were surrounded by shame and humiliation.

But God promised the Jews deliverance from shame! Let's see what the prophet Isaiah said about rebuilding the reputation of Zion.

Isaiah 54:1-4 KJV
[1] Sing, O barren, thou that didst not bear; break forth into singing, and cry aloud, thou that didst not travail with child: for more are the children of the desolate than the children of the married wife, saith the Lord. [2] Enlarge the

place of thy tent, and let them stretch forth the curtains of thine habitations: spare not, lengthen thy cords, and strengthen thy stakes; [3] For thou shalt break forth on the right hand and on the left; and thy seed shall inherit the Gentiles, and make the desolate cities to be inhabited. [4] Fear not; for thou shalt not be ashamed: neither be thou confounded; for thou shalt not be put to shame: for thou shalt forget the shame of thy youth, and shalt not remember the reproach of thy widowhood any more.

In this passage, God is speaking to Jerusalem as a widow, because Jerusalem had lost the covenant relationship that God had made to marry the land; Jerusalem had lost the covenant through death, through the sin that brought death. So in God's eyes, Jerusalem was a widow to be reproached for her actions that had led to the death of the covenant. But God said that Jerusalem would forget the shame of her youth, and no longer remember the reproach of her widowhood. Likewise, God promises us that He will remove shame from our lives and that we will get our reputation back, not for our glory, but so that His name will be glorified. Maybe we have had to face cruel words and mockery, but God is

> *MC+*
>
> *God promises us that He will remove shame from our lives and that we will get our reputation back, not for our glory, but so that His name will be glorified.*

restoring everything back. God is remembering His good word toward us, and He will perform it. God is releasing things that have been held up in the heavenlies, and bringing deliverance for our destinies.

Prayer

Dear Lord,

As You rebuild the ruins in my life, help me to rely on You to provide everything that I need. You are my Divine Protector, and I put my trust in You, not in man, to provide what I need. Thank You for taking the painful pieces of my life and building them into something beautiful. Give me the strength that I need to take back territory. In the name of Jesus, amen!

Dr. Michelle Corral

Diary for Destiny

1. What is the most devastated dream of your life? You may have experienced a divorce, financial crisis, death of a loved one, loss of reputation, or another devastated dream. Be honest with the Lord about the situation and your feelings.

_____

_____

_____

_____

_____

_____

2. How do you know that God will change your mourning into a miracle?

_____

_____

_____

_____

_____

_____

Chapter Two

Consolation In Your

Desolation
~Nehemiah Miracles~

Have you ever asked the question, "Why do bad things happen to good people?" Beloved, this is a very common question that arises out of our painful experiences. This question often arises because we see our suffering as an indictment from God. When we have been geared to think in a non-affirming, guilt-driven mindset, we begin looking for the reason why God let this happen. We don't know how to process our pain, so the first person we blame is ourselves. All of these inward anxieties trouble us because we see our suffering as something that could never be used for good or as something completely useless that happened for no reason.

Dr. Michelle Corral

The very first thing that must be established here is validation. We serve a God who places a very high price tag on your personal pain. Your personal pain is so precious to Him. Psalm 56:8 says, "Thou tellest my wanderings: put thou my tears into thy bottle: are they not in thy book?" Scripture is written in a way that validates our personal pain. In Genesis 29:31, the text teaches, "And when the Lord saw that Leah was hated, He opened her womb." In reality, Leah was not hated. The righteous patriarch Jacob truly loved Leah. However, he did not love her as much as he loved Rachel. Leah felt so rejected that to her it felt as if she was hated. Scripture records her reality because it validates and valuates her personal pain.

The Bible not only validates our personal pain, but also shows us that God compensates with great compassion. The text teaches that "He opened her [Leah's] womb." In Genesis 29:31, Leah's life shows us divine validation and divine compensation. In the book of Nehemiah, the text teaches us how God can take the pain of our past and rebuild the ruins. One of the themes of Ezra and Nehemiah is that the glory of the latter shall be greater than the former. This is the prophecy of Haggai 2:9, which occurred during the rebuilding periods of Ezra and Nehemiah.

Some of us have lost hope because we don't know how God can possibly make something that lies ahead better than the painful past of what once was. The book of

Nehemiah begins with the report given to Nehemiah, a great man of Israel who served as cupbearer to the king of Persia, concerning those that were left in the city of Zion after the burning. Nothing was left of the Temple. Only rubble and rubbish remained after the city was ransacked. All that remained of Zion was ash and broken down walls. In the city was a desolate population that was traumatized and immobilized from the setbacks of the devastating days of Nebuchadnezzar's invasion.

Nehemiah 1:2-3 KJV
[2] That Hanani, one of my brethren, came, he and certain men of Judah; and I asked them concerning the Jews that had escaped, which were left of the captivity, and concerning Jerusalem. [3] And they said unto me, The remnant that are left of the captivity there in the province are in great affliction and reproach: the wall of Jerusalem also is broken down, and the gates thereof are burned with fire.

MC+
No matter how devastating and dark the aftermath may appear, God will bring destiny out of it.

This text teaches that there was nothing left but ashes and ruins. In a literal sense, ashes are the minerals that remain after something has been burnt. Ashes represent the aftermath. The Bible shows us that no matter how devastating and dark the aftermath may appear, God will bring destiny out of it. The promise to you is that the latter shall be greater than the former.

Haggai 2:9 KJV
The glory of this latter house shall be greater than of the former, saith the Lord of hosts: and in this place will I give peace, saith the Lord of hosts.

At the same time that Nehemiah was sent to rebuild the ruins of Jerusalem and Haggai prophesied to the rebuilders, God also spoke to the prophet Ezekiel among the captives in Babylon.

Ezekiel 36:11 KJV
And I will multiply upon you man and beast; and they shall increase and bring fruit: and I will settle you after your old estates, and will do better unto you than at your beginnings: and ye shall know that I am the Lord.

God's promise to you is a "better than before" anointing. "I shall do better to you than in your beginning" (Ezekiel 36:11) was the word that God gave to Zion after the burning. Just as God promised a "better than before" anointing to the children of Israel, so God has promised you that there is hope through the Messiah. These days of trials and tribulation will come to an end. God promises you "better than your beginning," meaning that you will experience not only restoration but also compensation. Your life will be better than before.

Beloved, these texts reveal the compassion of a Father who understands how difficult this dilemma has been for you. God understands how painful this period of your life has been. He knows the memories, the anxieties, and the feeling of loss. This is why the Bible teaches us the following:

Psalm 103:13-14 KJV
[13] Like as a father pitieth his children, so the Lord pitieth them that fear him. [14] For he knoweth our frame; he remembereth that we are dust.

The word "frame" comes from the Hebrew word *yetser* (Strong's Hebrew 1336). Yetser is not only a word, but it is also a concept that relates to all of the basic emotions and experiences that form our personality structure. God knows the origin of every thought, fear, and anxiety. He knows why we have the thoughts that we think, and He knows the emotions that trigger our thoughts. He knows the very origins of our anxieties. He knows exactly how we began to become afraid or where a certain guilt-ridden anxiety or fear-based anxiety resides in our core.

The word yetser (as we see in "He knoweth our frame") indicates that God understands our personality structure.

In other words, His compassion is toward the place and the point where the pain began. The Bible reveals how compassionate your Father is toward the origin and point of your pain. That pain may have begun as a rejection hidden under the rubble of a dysfunctional childhood, or maybe that anxiety had its origin in abandonment issues that you might have been too young to deal with. These personal issues often have origins at the very base of our human need. For some of us, anxieties, fears, or little disorders or obsessions began when we were children as we took the shame or pain and buried it under all the stones when the dream collapsed or our security collapsed. This could have occurred because of a divorce, or through the death of a parent.

The Bible shows us how tenderly Jesus deals with the origin and point of our pain. In Mark 9, the text teaches that a man came to Jesus with a son who had a disorder that continually caused him to throw himself into fire and water. The father of the child tells Jesus that he knew the suffering of his child was of demonic origin. Then in Mark 9:21, Jesus asked the father, "How long is it ago since this came unto him? And he said, Of a child." Beloved, Jesus did not ask this question because He did not know. He asked this question for His disciples to know that when He is bringing deliverance, he begins at the point of our pain. He knows the moment our world changed. He compassionately validates the personal pain and understands how and why we stay stuck in our personality patterns. You may ask the question, "How do I know that my personal pain is precious to Him? How do I know that He not only validates but also promises to compensate all my broken dreams and burdens I have buried?"

In Leviticus 6:8-13, we see a portion of Torah called "Terumas haDeshen" in Hebrew. Terumas haDeshen translates from Hebrew to English as "the elevation of the ashes." This elevation of the ashes was the first priestly duty of the *cohen* (priest) every day before he dispatched the other duties of service. Every morning the priest would go to the evening sacrifice and get a handful of ashes and raise them to heaven, saying a special blessing over them.

MC+

He will bring elevation out of devastation. He will use all your pain toward His purpose.

I believe your Great High Priest has gone to your personal ashes, taken them, and elevated and consecrated your personal pain, promising that He will bring blessing out of your brokenness. He will bring elevation out of devastation. He will use all your pain toward His purposes.

Elevation out of your devastation is not only the personal prophetic promise of Terumas haDeshen from Leviticus 6:8-13, but Paul also teaches us in Romans 8:18, "For I reckon that the sufferings of this present time are not worthy to be compared with the glory which shall be revealed in us." Your ashes will be elevated and consecrated for your dream and destiny.

Beloved, the book of Nehemiah is a prophetic parallel of how the Holy Spirit takes our devastated dreams and uses them for destiny. Nehemiah is one of God's servants that prophetically prefigures the consolation and comfort given to us by the Holy Spirit. Have you ever wondered what the personality of the Holy Spirit is like? Have you ever wondered about what He really wants to do with you? Nehemiah, the great governor, left his position as the king's cupbearer (Nehemiah 1:11b: "I was the king's cupbearer") and led an expedition into Jerusalem to rebuild the ruins of the city.

"Cupbearer" also means "burden-bearer." The Holy Spirit truly is the burden-bearer for the King. He does this as the last line in Romans 8:26-27 says, "But the Spirit itself maketh intercession for us with groanings which cannot be uttered." Just as Nehemiah was the king's cupbearer, the Holy Spirit is a cupbearer of the King, presenting our deepest needs to the King, with groanings that cannot be uttered.

Nehemiah is a prophetic prototype of the Holy Spirit. The name Nehemiah means "the Lord comforts," just as the

Dr. Michelle Corral

Spirit of God is a comforter (John 14:7). As a type of comforter, Nehemiah shows us the true comfort of the Holy Spirit. Just as Nehemiah returned to rebuild the ruins of Jerusalem, so does the Holy Spirit reveal the ruins of our lives.

In Nehemiah 1:3, the text teaches that Nehemiah was concerned for the *peletah* (Strong's Hebrew 6413) of Jerusalem. The *peletah* are those who were left in Jerusalem when their Jewish brethren were taken into captivity by the Babylonians. The Hebrew word *peletah* indicates survival, and the *peletah* are those who have supernaturally survived the storm. In Jerusalem, the *peletah* were those who were still standing among the rubbish, the ruins, and the ash heap. They were eyewitnesses of the burning of the city of Zion. The memories of the *peletah* were filled with flashes of the tribes of Judah and Benjamin being taken captive, bowing under cruel chains on their way to Babylon.

Nehemiah 1:3 KJV
And they said unto me, The remnant that are left of the captivity there in the province are in great affliction and reproach: the wall of Jerusalem also is broken down, and the gates thereof are burned with fire.

Nehemiah was grieved and received permission to go and rebuild the ruins of Jerusalem, an endeavor that was

Dr. Michelle Corral

completely financed by the king of Persia. Nehemiah returned to Zion and found that it was dark, broken, desolated, and in rubble. So Nehemiah did a sanctification of the name of God, or a *Kiddush Hashem*. He approached the city at night with only a few guards so that no one would see him, and entered Zion through the dung gate, or rubbish gate. Nehemiah could have entered through any of the city's 12 gates, but he chose to enter through the dung gate.

Nehemiah began to look through the dung and rubbish, and began to weep over the stones. When Nehemiah started to rebuild the ruins, even though he had access to new stones and all the finances he needed, he chose to use the stones that were under the ash heap. Nehemiah lifted the stones to heaven and said a *bracha* (blessing) over every stone, then placed the stones back into the wall.

Nehemiah is a prototype of how the Holy Spirit enters into our broken dreams, our rubbish, our ruins, and ash heaps, and begins to rebuild; He looks for refuse and rubble that He can use for purpose in the midst of our pain. As in the case of Nehemiah, the rebuilding project is financed by the King and is fully paid for by the blood of Jesus. The Holy Spirit's role as Comforter is to rebuild the ruins and search for the stones that have been marred and charred, and buried under the rubble. These stones are the pieces of your pain that will be placed inside the wall, and used as part of God's design of destiny in your life.

God Will Use Our Painful Pieces To Rebuild Our Ruins

Rebuilding of the ruins happens when God takes the pieces of our pain and turns them into purpose. Just like Nehemiah took stones that were burned and broken to rebuild the walls of Jerusalem, so will God take the painful parts of our lives and use them to rebuild our purpose and our destiny.

Nehemiah 4:1-2 KJV
[1] But it came to pass, that when Sanballat heard that we builded the wall, he was wroth, and took great indignation, and mocked the Jews. [2] And he spake before his brethren and the army of Samaria, and said, What do these feeble Jews? will they fortify themselves? will they sacrifice? will they make an end in a day? will they revive the stones out of the heaps of the rubbish which are burned?

Sanballat and those with him were mocking Nehemiah because he was sanctifying and blessing the stones that he had taken from the heaps of rubbish. Nehemiah used the burned and charred stones, those that were under the rubble and were considered useless, and he found a place for them.

Similarly, God used the jewels of silver and the jewels of gold that the children of Israel brought forth out of Egypt to build the Tabernacle. The jewels of silver and the jewels of gold represent the years of tears that the children of Israel suffered in Egypt. The jewels of silver and the jewels of gold were their divine compensation for all their devastation. These jewels were used to build the Ark of the Covenant, the menorah, the table of shew bread, and everything holy in the Tabernacle. These are a spiritual

MC+

The Holy Spirit is not looking for perfect vessels. He is looking for bruised and broken vessels. This is how He uses our pain to train for greatness.

similitude of how God will take the years of your tears and use them for His glory. This is exactly what God did with the burned stones in the city of Jerusalem. He chose the burnt and marred stones to be put in the wall. The Holy Spirit is not looking for perfect vessels. He is looking for bruised and broken vessels. This is how He uses our pain to train for greatness.

Power Principles in Nehemiah for Taking Back Territory

Beloved, in the time of *Shivat Zion*, there are four power principles that we can apply to our lives for taking back territory from the enemy.

Power Principle 1: Taking Possession Requires Divine Intercession of the Holy Spirit on Our Behalf

Nehemiah 1:11 KJV
O Lord, I beseech thee, let now thine ear be attentive to the prayer of thy servant, and to the prayer of thy servants, who desire to fear thy name: and prosper, I pray thee, thy servant this day, and grant him mercy in the sight of this man. For I was the king's cupbearer.

As we saw earlier, Nehemiah represents the work of the Holy Spirit in a powerful way, because the Holy Spirit is the burdenbearer of our ruins. While Jesus intercedes for us in heaven, the Holy Spirit intercedes for us on earth through the physical body of every individual in the body of Christ. There may be times when we don't know how to pray, but when we let the Holy Spirit pray through us, our prayers will be answered.

Power Principle 2: Present the Superiority of God's Authority in His Word to the Enemy

Nehemiah 2:4-7 KJV
[4] Then the king said unto me, For what dost thou make request? So I prayed to the God of heaven. [5] And I said unto the king, If it please the king, and if thy servant have found favour in thy sight, that thou wouldest send me unto Judah, unto the city of my fathers' sepulchres, that I may build it. [6] And the king said unto me, (the queen also sitting by him,) For how long shall thy journey be? and when wilt thou return? So it pleased the king to send me; and I set him a time. [7] Moreover I said unto the king, If it please the king, let letters be given me to the governors beyond the river, that they may convey me over till I come into Judah.

Just as Nehemiah brought letters from the king to give to the governors in Jerusalem, we are going to need the written Word from the King in order to rebuild the ruins in our lives and fulfill our destinies. We need to know what the written Word of God says about us and our destinies, and we will need to present this Word written on our behalf to enemy principalities in order to enter the Promised Land and take back territory.

Power Principle 3: We Must Press Past Opposition In Order To Transition Into The Place That God Has For Us

Nehemiah 4:1-2 KJV
[1] But it came to pass, that when Sanballat heard that we built the wall, he was wroth, and took great indignation, and mocked the Jews. [2] And he spake before his brethren and the army of Samaria, and said, What do these feeble Jews? will they fortify themselves? will they sacrifice? will they make an end in a day? will they revive the stones out of the heaps of the rubbish which are burned?

We need to understand that we will be in for a fight, and that we will need the supernatural anointing of God to press all the way to the end and get back everything that the enemy has stolen out of our lives. The Israelites who went back to Zion didn't have weapons such as bows, arrows, or spears like Joshua did; they didn't go into battle with large armies. Instead, they used spiritual weapons and pressed past the opposition through a one-on-one tearing down of imaginations, taking dominion over strongholds, stopping accusations, pressing past discouragement, and battling the witchcraft of words. We need to have an attitude that says, "I am not going to take this!" We need God's persistence against the resistance. If we have to go on a Daniel fast for seven

MC+
We need God's persistence against the resistance.

years, or get up early and go on our faces to get our children back, or our ministries back, and believe God for the impossible, we can't be intimidated. We just have to do it, by the grace of God!

We have to *want* to get our dreams back. Some of us are comfortable with captivity and have accepted it as a way of life. Coming out of captivity begins with our attitudes. We cannot settle for compromise or comfort in captivity; we must not receive what the enemy is offering us. We must refuse to settle for anything less than God's best!

Power Principle 4: The Resurrection As God's Reflection for Rebuilding the Ruins in Our Lives

We need to understand the resurrection of our Lord before we can begin rebuilding the ruins in our lives. There is a Calvary connection in every book of the Bible. Whenever we see miracles, we will see a supernatural symbol of the Messiah. It is through Jesus Christ that we possess the promises of God. Even though He has been despised and rejected of men, and not received by His own brethren, He is the hope of Israel, the Messiah.

The perfection of resurrection is one of the greatest supernatural secrets of how God is the "Rebuilder of Our Ruins." In Nehemiah 2:11-12a, the text teaches that just before Nehemiah entered the city, he waited for three days.

Nehemiah 2:11-12a KJV
[11] So I came to Jerusalem, and was there three days.
[12] And I arose in the night.

The symbol of three days is a prophetic parallel to the miraculous manifestation of the third day. It prefigures the power of Jesus' resurrection. Nehemiah 2:12 says, "I arose in the night." The context conveys God's guarantee that He will resurrect our ruins; it is a reflection of the Resurrection in our own lives. God has given His guarantee that He will rebuild the ruins: that promise has been bought by the blood!

Prayer

Father, I receive the anointing to press past the opposition in order to transition to take the territory back. I rebuke and bind every spirit that's in the land illegally. I take back my territory. I bind the mocking spirit and the witchcraft of words. I bind the spirit of discouragement and the spirit of situations that look impossible, that make me want to give up. I will fight until I get back every promise that God has given me. In the name of Jesus, amen!

Diary for Destiny

1. Has there ever been a time in your life when you saw the Lord take something that was broken and charred, and turn it into something beautiful, either in your own life or in the life of someone that you know? Describe what happened. God is a God of hope and restoration; know that what He has done before, He is able to do again.

_____

_____

_____

_____

_____

2. What are some areas of your life that are marred and charred, burnt and broken, like the stones that Nehemiah used to rebuild the wall? Right now, invite the Lord into those painful areas and ask Him to do something amazing with the painful pieces in your life.

_____

_____

_____

_____

_____

Dr. Michelle Corral

Do whatever the Lord is leading you to do in order to help turn these ashes into something beautiful. You may need to forgive yourself or other people, and take practical steps to amend a situation like writing a letter of apology, or spending time with a family member or friend who has been needing to talk with you. Most importantly, spend time with the Lord and in His Word; He will continue the rebuilding process in your life.

Dr. Michelle Corral

Chapter Three

Holding On To Hope

Tikvateinu ("Our Hope") is a poetic masterpiece written in 1877 by the award-winning poet Naphtali Herz Imber. *Tikvatienu* expresses the hope of God's promise to Zion concerning rebuilding and reclaiming after years of tears and a long, dark exile. *Tikvateinu* expresses the ability that God has given every soul who trusts Him to continue to hope even in the midst of unbearable human suffering and circumstances. This incredible expression of hope and trust in God's eternal love and compassion became fulfilled in 1948 by the founding of the state of Israel. I believe the fullness of that expression of hope was demonstrated as a revered living legacy during the Holocaust. In 1944, Czech Jews heroically sang *Tikvateinu* (now called *Hatikvah*) as they entered into the stench-filled chambers of death at the Auschwitz-Birkenau gas chambers.

Tikvateinu was courageously sung as these heroes of hope expressed their trust and belief that God's faithfulness to Zion is eternal. These heroes of hope were witnesses that God would rebuild, restore, and give back the land that He had promised, which came to pass four years after their death. Although we have never been through a Holocaust, each one of us has storms and sufferings in this life. Every one of us has been challenged with our own disappointed dreams or sudden storms that came out of nowhere.

Through many years in ministry, I have heard stories of those who "came back" after their crisis because of God's faithfulness to fulfill His promises of restoration after devastation. Throughout the Bible, the text teaches how God raises up heroes that give us hope. These heroes of hope have one common denominator of destiny: overcoming storms.

Storms are a prophetic prefiguring of grievous trials and tribulations in our lives. Storms by nature come upon us suddenly. Recently in California, we had 90 degree temperatures, followed by sudden storms the next day out of nowhere.

In Acts 27:13, the text teaches how suddenly a storm came upon a ship that the apostle Paul was traveling on, which had set sail with smooth waters and clear, calm skies: "And when the south wind blew softly, supposing that they had obtained their purpose, loosing thence, they sailed close by Crete."

But the next verse shows us that, without warning, a fierce storm like no other came upon Paul and the others on the ship.

Acts 27:14 KJV
But not long after there arose against it a tempestuous wind, called Euroclydon.

In the remainder of Acts 27, the text teaches that day after day, Paul and the men on the ship were faced with a fight that seemed impossible to survive. Some of us right now are facing that same fight. We are doing everything possible to survive the storm. Storm survival can take so much out of us that we are so drained that we can't even think about destiny. God wants you to know that it is not your destiny to stay stuck in this storm. God wants you to know that there is hope. He has given it to you as He gave it to Zion. God promised Zion as God has promised you that "there is hope in thine end" (Jeremiah 31:17). This means that there is hope in your future. This is a season of storms,

> *MC+*
> *This is a season of storms, but if you can survive the storm by holding on to the hope, you will see your success.*

but if you can survive the storm by holding on to the hope, you will see your success.

The prophetic word given to Zion after the city was burnt to ashes is given as a hope to us for our shattered destinies and dreams, as we see in the book of Lamentations:

Lamentations 3:17b-18 KJV
[17b] I forgat prosperity. [18] And I said, My strength and my hope is perished from the Lord.

Lamentations 3:21-24 KJV
[21] This I recall to my mind, therefore have I hope. [22] It is of the Lord's mercies that we are not consumed, because his compassions fail not. [23] They are new every morning: great is thy faithfulness. [24] The Lord is my portion, saith my soul; therefore will I hope in him.

Beloved, this is your anchor and your hope: God's faithfulness will see you through the storm and bring you to success. The ruins will be restored. All of your pain will be used to train for greatness.

MC+
God's faithfulness will see you through the storm and bring you to success. The ruins will be restored. All of your pain will be used to train for greatness.

You may ask the question, "How does God connect my pain to my purpose?" Connecting pain to purpose is one of the ways that the power of providence works in our lives. The power of providence is the hidden hand of God directing and connecting our darkest days to our destiny. This promise of destiny out of our darkness is the first miracle in the Bible, as we see in the book of Genesis:

Genesis 1:2-3 KJV
The earth was without form, and void; and darkness was upon the face of the deep. And God said, Let there be light: and there was light.

The Hebrew word for light, *ohr*, is not just the absence of darkness. *Ohr* also means hope, deliverance, and breakthrough. In this text, God brought light (*ohr*) or destiny out of the darkness. Genesis 1:2-3 prophetically prefigures how God brings a plan out of a painful past. This is how He connects purpose to our pain.

You may feel that your devastation could never experience total restoration. You may feel that you cannot see any possible purpose behind what has happened to you. You may feel so confused, and that your destiny is shattered and scattered. This is how the children of Israel felt: Scripture validates the feelings of Zion after the destruction of both the northern and southern kingdoms.

Dr. Michelle Corral

Connecting Pain With Purpose

Ezekiel 37:1-6 KJV
[1] The hand of the Lord was upon me, and carried me out in the spirit of the Lord, and set me down in the midst of the valley which was full of bones, [2] And caused me to pass by them round about: and, behold, there were very many in the open valley; and, lo, they were very dry. [3] And he said unto me, Son of man, can these bones live? And I answered, O Lord God, thou knowest. [4] Again he said unto me, Prophesy upon these bones, and say unto them, O ye dry bones, hear the word of the Lord. [5] Thus saith the Lord God unto these bones; Behold, I will cause breath to enter into you, and ye shall live: [6] And I will lay sinews upon you, and will bring up flesh upon you, and cover you with skin, and put breath in you, and ye shall live; and ye shall know that I am the Lord.

In this vision of the valley of dry bones, Ezekiel saw bones that were scattered everywhere. The bones were scattered throughout the valley, making it impossible to tell if it was a human being or even a single entity of any kind. The hand bones were in one place, the foot bones were in another place; nothing was connected. Was this a human being? What were these bones? What did they represent? They had no flesh and no sinews upon them. They were just bones that were very dry.

Dr. Michelle Corral

First of all, we need to understand that these bones represent the entire house of Israel being in a state of captivity. These bones represent what happened to the core of Israel through the Assyrian captivity and later the Babylonian captivity. Israel had become a nation that was scattered and shattered. The Assyrian captivity took the northern 10 tribes of Israel and scattered them to the ends of the earth, and the Babylonian captivity took captive the southern kingdom of the tribes of Judah and Benjamin, and brought them to Babylon.

The spiritual state of the dry bones is a vision that validates and valuates our sense of confusion and calamity and lack of clarity in the aftermath of something very traumatizing. The context conveys compassion to individuals who have gone through a shocking reality loss in their lives. Scripture is rendering relevance to every person who has gone through a time in their lives when they felt completely displaced and disconnected because tragedy detoured their dreams into an impossible place. This might be a widow who doesn't know where to begin picking up the pieces of her life, and has only memories left. This might be a man who spent years pouring his talent and time into a company that collapsed without warning; one day he had an incredible career and the next day he had to deal with the shock of the storm. How does God connect pain and purpose?

Scripture is talking about personal pain because God wants us to know that our pain is relevant to Him. What we have been through is of great price and value to God. God knows what it's like to have gone through the shocking circumstances that many of us have been through. Sometimes it's so difficult to sort out the pieces and try to connect the dots again. But the God we serve is a bone connector. He is able to take the pieces of your pain and connect it to your purpose.

He can connect everything you've ever been through in your past and connect it to the prophecies and promises He has given you. Ezekiel 37:7 reveals the Lord as our "Divine Connector." He connects tragedy to triumph. He connects disappointment to destiny. He connects pain to purpose. He connects destiny to the darkest day of our life.

Ezekiel 37:7 KJV
So I prophesied as I was commanded: and as I prophesied, there was a noise, and behold a shaking, and the bones came together, bone to his bone.

God is saying to you, "All the pain of your past is being connected to purpose." I'm not going to leave you in a valley of dry bones scattered without an identity, without

MC+

God is saying to you, "All the pain of your past is being connected to purpose."

any purpose. I am going to take every piece of your pain and connect it. I'm bringing you to a place where everything you've ever been through in your life will have a design of destiny." God is going to put all the pieces of our pain together; we will see that everything had a purpose and that God will use our pain for the highest dimension of destiny in our lives.

Right now we may not understand how God really sees our personal pain, and how He identifies with the feelings that are so scattered. We may be biologically alive, but we have stopped "living." This tragedy took the life from us. There is a word in the Hebrew language for someone who is alive with purpose and has the life of God's breath in them, and that word is *chaim* – it's the word for "life." Similarly, the word *zoe* in Greek means having purpose and focus. When we go through the motions of living without life, it is a sign that we have lost our hope, our *chaim*, our *zoe*. We can see this is how the children of Israel felt in Ezekiel 37.

Ezekiel 37:11 KJV
Then he said unto me, Son of man, these bones are the whole house of Israel: behold, they say, Our bones are dried, and our hope is lost: we are cut off for our parts.

But God told Ezekiel to breathe upon the bones to bring them back to life!

Dr. Michelle Corral

Ezekiel 37:9 KJV
Then said he unto me, Prophesy unto the wind, prophesy,
son of man, and say to the wind, Thus saith the Lord God;
Come from the four winds, O breath, and breathe upon
these slain, that they may live.

We need to understand that when God told Ezekiel to
"breathe upon these bones," He meant: "Prophesy the
word of the living God upon these bones; I will cause
breath to come into them and they shall live." The word
ruach which is translated in these verses as "breath" also
means "anointing." God is saying that He will cause the
Holy Spirit to come into us, and we will live. This is the
prophetic process that God uses to bring us back into our
place and position. This is how He raises the ruins, and gets
us up out of the pit into a position of praise.

Ezekiel 37:12 KJV
Therefore prophesy and say unto them, Thus saith the Lord
God; Behold, O my people, I will open your graves, and
cause you to come up out of your graves, and bring you
into the land of Israel.

This is the promise to take back territory. You will again
repossess the promises of taken territory. When Ezekiel
prophesied the prophetic word upon the bones, he saw a
miraculous manifestation of divine restoration. That's how
the prophetic word works: it brings the *Ruach* (Holy Spirit)

and the anointing into our lives. It pulls us out of the pit and puts us on the land. It brings us into our destiny and into the promised place that God has ordained for us.

The prophetic word also restores our hope, our *tikvah* in the Hebrew language. We need to understand that hope in a Biblical sense does not mean just wishing for something to happen. Some of us have this concept and say things like, "I wish this would happen! I hope this will turn out a certain way." No, hope is an expectancy that something *will* happen. There's no "if" involved in hope. Biblical hope means that the only thing between our current circumstances and what we are hoping for is time and the power of His providence to work it out.

Let's take a look at the first time that the word *tikvah* (hope) is used in the Bible. The first time that a word appears in the Bible is important, because all subsequent uses of that word are related to the meaning of the word the first time that it appeared. The word *tikvah* first appears in Joshua 2, but it is not used in the sense of hoping for something; instead, the meaning of *tikvah* in Joshua 2 is "cord" or "thread." Joshua told Rahab the harlot to let down a scarlet cord from her window, which would save her and her family when the Israelites took back the city of Jericho. That cord, or *tikvah*, was red or scarlet, to represent the fact that our hope is in the blood of Yeshua; it was a scarlet thread of hope and deliverance.

Dr. Michelle Corral

Joshua 2:17-18 KJV
[17] And the men said unto her, We will be blameless of
this thine oath which thou hast made us swear. [18]
Behold, when we come into the land, thou shalt bind this
line of scarlet thread [tikvah] in the window which thou
didst let us down by: and thou shalt bring thy father, and
thy mother, and thy brethren, and all thy father's
household, home unto thee.

Rahab hid and protected Joshua and Caleb when they first came to Jericho to spy out the land, so she made them swear that the Israelites would not harm her or her family when they came back to invade Jericho. In response, Joshua told her to bind a scarlet cord (*tikvah*) in the window as a sign of protection and promise. Any subsequent use of the word *tikvah* or "hope" in the Bible refers back to this appearance of the scarlet thread; when we hope for something, we have an expectation that it will happen based on the blood-bought covenant of Jesus on the cross. We need to understand that *Shivat Zion* is a season of Messianic miracles in our lives, and that the theme of *Shivat Zion* is hope! Our God is a God who is going to raise up our ruins. He is bringing great restoration in every place of desolation in our lives.

Prayer

Lord, I give You praise and I give You glory! Thank You for taking the pieces of my pain and connecting them with my purpose, and for connecting my past with my future! Help me to stand on the promises of Your Word, and to walk in a "nothing but God" season! I plead the blood of Yeshua in every area of my life, amen!

Diary for Destiny

1. Where have you lost hope in your life? Is there an area in your life that is so confused that you can't connect it to your purpose? Ask the Lord to begin to reveal to you how He will connect pain to purpose in your life.

_____

_____

_____

_____

_____

2. What can you see from your past that has paved the path of your future?

_____

_____

_____

_____

_____

Chapter Four

Your Comeback After Your Crisis

A torn and shredded coat dipped in the blood of a goat was brought to Jacob by his sons on that dark and desolate day. "This we have found, know now whether it be thy son's coat or no" (Genesis 37:32b). With horror and unbelief in Jacob's eyes, the cruel reality takes precedence over his denial. Pressing his fingers over the coat in an effort to resist this horrifying reality, he immediately knows without a shadow of doubt that it is his son Joseph's coat. Instantaneously, Jacob plummets to the ground and the sounds of crying, wailing, and the tearing of garments erupt throughout the camp. The smell of dust rises in the air as God's beloved servant Jacob, whose spiritual name is Israel, covers his head with ashes and dust. Wailing and weeping break out in travail for both Jacob and Joseph.

Genesis 37:34-35 KJV
[34] And Jacob rent his clothes, and put sackcloth upon his loins, and mourned for his son many days. [35] And all his sons and all his daughters rose up to comfort him; but he refused to be comforted; and he said, For I will go down into the grave unto my son mourning. Thus his father wept for him.

In reality, Joseph was not dead, but Jacob had no idea that his beloved son was still alive. The shredded coat dipped in the blood of a goat was seemingly undeniable evidence. It was Joseph's coat, and it was shred to pieces. There was no doubt in Jacob's mind that some wild beast had devoured Joseph and that he was dead. Scripture says, "And he knew it, and said, It is my son's coat; an evil beast hath devoured him; Joseph is without doubt rent in pieces" (Genesis 37:33 KJV). The shredded coat was ripped in pieces. This was the garment (the godly raiment) that was a sign of Joseph's firstborn status as Rachel's firstborn son that she bore to Jacob. This coat provided a visible identity that Joseph was the heir to the Abrahamic covenant. This coat solidified the status of Joseph's position among his brethren. This coat represented the dreams that someday Joseph's brethren would bow down before him and finally recognize that this status and special place as rightful heir to the Abrahamic covenant that set him in firstborn status was given to him by God and not by man. But now, this coat of many colors was so tattered, torn, and stained with blood that it was almost unrecognizable.

Joseph's coat is a prophetic parallel to every dreamer who has hopes and aspirations, and believes that God has a great destiny that was ordained before the foundations of the world for them. Sometimes, beloved, that coat is the cause of great controversy in our lives. The coat represents the destiny that God has given us. For some of us, the battles and warfare involved in possessing the promises that God has given us have been so intense that we have started to lose hope that our dreams really are a God-given reality that will surely come to pass.

The torn and tattered coat prophetically parallels a destiny that has been devastated by unforeseen circumstances. It represents what once was that now is torn up, shattered, and tattered by something we were not expecting. It represents our inabilities and human frailties that cannot turn back the clock and avoid unforeseen circumstances that have changed our lives forever.

How God Uses Pain To Train For Greatness

Jacob's pain was more excruciating than what we can imagine. Jacob is the one who had already sensed in his heart and knew the intense animosity of Joseph's brothers toward him. Yet on that dark day, it was Jacob who sent Joseph to Shechem knowing in the back of his mind how Joseph's brothers hated him, which was evident in their constant rejection of him.

Genesis 37:13 KJV
And Israel said unto Joseph, Do not thy brethren feed the flock in Shechem? come, and I will send thee unto them. And he said to him, Here am I.

It was Jacob who sent Joseph to that place (Shechem), not knowing that Joseph would not return home or that he would not see Joseph's face again for many years. Beloved, so often we ask ourselves the question, "How could I have been so stupid as to make a decision like that?" or "Why didn't I pay attention to the warning signs?" We say, "If only I had known better. Dear God, why did this happen? If I had only known things would end up like this, then I would have never made that decision. Why, Lord, why?" We blame ourselves over something that we had no control over. Beloved, here Scripture comforts those of us who cannot turn back the hands of time. We go on blaming ourselves and carrying great burdens of unresolved pain and guilt for things that were out of our control. These texts are showing us this so that we know that all things work together for good for those who love God and are called according to His purpose (see Romans 8:28).

In this passage, the Bible changes Jacob's name and inserts use of his spiritual name instead. The verse says, "Israel said to Joseph," not "Jacob said to Joseph" (see Genesis 37:13). The context conveys this in a very methodical way for a purpose. First, it is presented this way for the sake of God's sovereignty. Scripture wants us to know that what we may perceive to be a terrible or tragic thing that happened to Joseph was truly a part of God's great plan of providence. What we are going to see is a torn coat. This torn coat represents the dilemmas that have devastated our dreams.

Our perception of certain predicaments is that they are hopeless, like the torn coat. It appears to be completely tragic without a trace of anything that could be of possible use toward a dream or destiny. Our situation appears as if nothing can redeem the dream. These excruciating issues around the coat are now brought into another level of unresolved guilt when we identity with what must have been in Jacob's mind. He was probably thinking, "Why did I send Joseph to Shechem?" This becomes something that the text wants us to see so that future generations that read these verses can receive hope and comfort, as we are able to identity with both Joseph and also Jacob. This is done through a very deliberate literary device employed by the text that exchanges the name Jacob for Israel. This is done so that we would know that God takes our painful mistakes and turns them into miracles.

Jacob represents humanness and frailties. Israel was his spiritual name that was given to him by God in Genesis 35 and in Genesis 32:28. When Scripture uses this spiritual name, it is showing us that what is being done or decided upon was ordered by God. In this case, it was the power of providence that led Israel to say to Joseph, "I will send thee to Shechem." Scripture changes the usual name of Jacob to Israel so we will know that this was a divine decision ordered by heaven and given to Jacob. He was inspired by God to make the decision to send Joseph to Shechem. This is written to help us understand that sometimes God allows or even inspires us to do certain things, just like He did here with Jacob.

God had a plan behind the sale of Joseph into slavery. It was a plan so great that it could not be compared to the glory that would be revealed in the outcome. God wants you to know that a plan will come out of your situation, like it did for Jacob concerning Joseph.

Genesis 50:18-20 KJV
[18] And his brethren also went and fell down before his face; and they said, Behold, we be thy servants. [19] And Joseph said unto them, Fear not: for am I in the place of God? [20] But as for you, ye thought evil against me; but God meant it unto good, to bring to pass, as it is this day, to save much people alive.

Beloved, what a plan God had behind all of these painful and unresolved issues. In Genesis 50:20, Joseph is speaking kindly to his brethren who so cruelly sold him into slavery. He comforts them by saying that God had a plan behind this pain. The plan was to not only save the seed of Abraham, but also thousands of other lives during the worldwide famine. This dilemma became God's plan to produce a great destiny for Joseph. The way that God worked for Joseph, He will work for you. God wants you to know that He will redeem your dream and use your dilemma for destiny. The way that God brings His plan out of our pain is prophetically paralleled in Genesis 37:28. On the dark day that Joseph was sold into slavery, he was put on a caravan of Ishmaelites. In a very irregular sense, the text goes out if its way to document the details of the goods that were hidden in the caravan. The questions should be asked: Why does Scripture give us details about what's in the caravan? Aren't we focusing on the shock of the sale and the deep rejection and personal pain that Joseph is bearing at the moment? Why do we care what is in the caravan?

The text goes out of its way to describe the details in the caravan not just so we know it happened, but also to teach us that what was on the caravan prophetically parallels God's plan, purpose, and power in Joseph's life. This shows the prophetic agenda of Moses conveyed in concept to every generation that needs it.

Dr. Michelle Corral

Genesis 37:25 KJV
And they sat down to eat bread: and they lifted up their eyes and looked, and, behold, a company of Ishmeelites came from Gilead with their camels bearing spicery and balm and myrrh, going to carry it down to Egypt.

In a literal sense of Scripture, bearing spicery, balm, and myrrh is a direct connect to Exodus 30:23-31. The text teaches us here about the principles of power in the anointing. And this passage also conveys to us that the principal spices, the myrrh, and the other spices are the primary properties in the anointing.

Exodus 30:23-24,31 KJV
[23] Take thou also unto thee principal spices, of pure myrrh five hundred shekels, and of sweet cinnamon half so much, even two hundred and fifty shekels, and of sweet calamus two hundred and fifty shekels, [24] And of cassia five hundred shekels, after the shekel of the sanctuary, and of oil olive an hin: [31] And thou shalt speak unto the children of Israel, saying, This shall be an holy anointing oil unto me throughout your generations.

In Genesis 37:25, the text is teaching us that the darkest day in Joseph's life is going to be used for destiny. The text is teaching that the grief, the shock, the despair, and the loss are the price behind the power that God is going to give to Joseph. It represents how God produces the power of the anointing in our lives. The spices and myrrh in Genesis 37:25 prophetically parallel how Joseph is going to reach a supernatural stratosphere of success in Egypt through the anointing. The anointing is a crucial component in Joseph's destiny. The comparison of Exodus 30:23-24 to Genesis 37:25 is made to demonstrate the price behind the power of God in his life.

In ancient Biblical times, spices were a commodity worth an equivalent of thousands of dollars. Among the spices found in the Middle East, myrrh was the most expensive. In those days, liquid myrrh was measured by the drop, which resembled a teardrop. Even though Joseph appeared to be going down into the darkness of Egypt alone, in actuality he was not going down there alone at all. He was going down into the depths of despair with the anointing!

Here the text is teaching us the price of power in the anointing. Joseph's future teaches us how God uses every test toward the best. Myrrh is the best of all the spices. In the future, Joseph is going to run the country of Egypt through the anointing that rests upon his life. This represents the price behind the power of God that will rest on his life. There is a comfort in the context when we understand that our pain is the price that God uses to train us for greatness.

The text teaches us that the anointing contains in it the power property of preservation, no matter how excruciating the tribulation is in your life. 1 Peter 1:5 uses the expression: "who are kept by the power of God." "Kept by the power of God" is a demonstration of the preserving power of God. This means that the anointing will keep you and preserve you through everything that seems humanly impossible to survive, and you will be able to remain standing. Jude 1:24 says, "Now unto him that is able to keep you from falling, and to present you faultless before the presence of his glory with exceeding joy."

The Power Property Of Preservation In All Your Tribulation

In Biblical times, myrrh was an incredibly expensive spice that was used in burials. It was known as a preservative. It prophetically prefigures the preserving power of God in the anointing. Through this, the text teaches that it is the anointing with this property of power for preservation during all your tribulation that will keep you throughout the darkest, most difficult days of your life. Scripture is teaching us how Joseph was able to see success under such duress because of the anointing.

Genesis 39:1-2 KJV
[1] And Joseph was brought down to Egypt; and Potiphar, an officer of Pharaoh, captain of the guard, an Egyptian, bought him of the hands of the Ishmeelites, which had brought him down thither. [2] And the Lord was with Joseph, and he was a prosperous man; and he was in the house of his master the Egyptian.

Myrrh also prophetically prefigures the perfection of resurrection in our lives. Myrrh is that property of power in the anointing that will give us the strength to "bounce back." This means there will be a comeback after the crisis in our lives through the principal spice of myrrh in the anointing. Scripture places the spicery, balm, and myrrh in a preface position in the text. It is positioned this way in the text prior to the difficult dilemmas that Joseph will face in Egypt to demonstrate that it was the preserving power of God in the anointing that kept Joseph during the most difficult days of his life.

The concept of bouncing back or making a comeback after a crisis is the primary theme in the Genesis account of Joseph's life. He presses his way and endures every day with hope based on his dreams. The ability to bounce back or come back after a crisis is a type of resurrection. This is another property of power in myrrh that demonstrates the perfection of resurrection in the anointing.

John 19:39-40 KJV
[39] And there came also Nicodemus, which at the first came to Jesus by night, and brought a mixture of myrrh and aloes, about an hundred pound weight. [40] Then took they the body of Jesus, and wound it in linen clothes with the spices, as the manner of the Jews is to bury.

Beloved, all you may have left of your dream may be as rubble amongst the ruins. But God wants you to know that if you have the anointing, you will come back after the crisis. You will bounce back like Joseph who came up out of the prison into the palace. You will rise again like Joseph. Joseph underwent a complete transformation for the new inauguration. This is a great example of a type of comeback after the crisis.

> *MC+*
> *God wants you to know that if you have the anointing, you will come back after the crisis.*

One of the greatest examples of how it is possible to come back after a crisis is seen in the life of Kathryn Kuhlman. Kathryn Kuhlman was a very successful woman preacher in the 1940s. She began her career at age 16 while traveling with her older sister and her evangelist husband. Later she became the pastor of a great church. During her years as a pastor, she made a huge mistake. As a result of her indiscretions, she fell into sin.

She lost her anointing. She lost her reputation and she lost her church. Her dream collapsed. The only thing left of a promising career was ashes. Kathryn repented and did everything in her power to try to get back what she had lost. God indeed forgave her, but to regain the place that she once had was almost impossible for a woman preacher in the 1940s.

Year after year, Kathryn did everything in her power to return to preaching. This became almost impossible, because everywhere she went the word somehow got out of her marred reputation and the pastors of the churches cancelled her invitations. Engagement after engagement was continually cancelled. She was humiliated, discouraged, and broken-hearted. This unfortunate situation went on for years. Everywhere she attempted to rebuild her ruins, someone would find out about her mistake and she would be cancelled.

After almost 15 years of anticipating her break and everything starting to look good, it would get out again. Tears were indeed Kathryn's bread. Her enemies were more numerous than the hairs on her head. Her life and ministry seemed almost impossible to remedy, but she still continued to trust that someday she would see a change and get her dream back.

Eventually, Kathryn moved her ministry to another state,

and attempted to rebuild her dream in Pittsburgh. After 15 years, Kathryn Kuhlman finally began to see a change, and this time everything was different. She began to pack the auditoriums. In the process of rebuilding the ruins in Pittsburgh, an unknown postman retrieved a letter from the post office addressed to one of the local pastors of Pittsburgh that would have ended her comeback immediately. Like spiritual Jerusalem, Kathryn had favor over her life.

Immediately after these things, an unusual occurrence began to happen in the life and ministry of Kathryn Kuhlman. Even though Kathryn wasn't specifically praying for the sick, miracles started to occur. One lady in her Pittsburgh meetings testified, "Miss Kuhlman, the tumor left my breast when you were preaching last night." Another said, "Miss Kuhlman, while you were preaching, my back was healed." The rest is history.

Kathryn Kuhlman ascended to heights no other preacher of her era could even imagine. After years of being denied, her destiny was finally released with a comeback unlike any other. Thousands began to flock to her meetings, often with more people outside than inside. At that time, Kathryn Kuhlman regained a reputation so integrous that few have ever been known among men or women with such a reputation of honor.

When I studied the works of the Holy Spirit under her influence, I had no idea at all until after her death what had happened. Kathryn Kuhlman became the greatest apostle of the Holy Spirit in the 20th century. Her life demonstrates that it is possible to come back after a crisis. God will rebuild your ruins. If He did it for Kathryn, He will do it for you.

The life of Kathryn Kuhlman shows us a God who gives us double for our shame, as we see in Isaiah 61:7.

Isaiah 61:7 KJV
For your shame ye shall have double; and for confusion they shall rejoice in their portion: therefore in their land they shall possess the double: everlasting joy shall be unto them.

He is the God who brings divine compensation for all our tribulation.

Beloved reader, I truly believe, if you have the anointing, God will do for you what He did for Joseph and for Kathryn Kuhlman. In your tribulation, you will experience preservation. The anointing will give you the power to bounce back and come back after your crisis. Let us be willing to pay the price for the anointing.

Dr. Michelle Corral

Kathryn Kuhlman said that there is a price to the anointing. It doesn't come cheap. She would say with her long skinny finger extended in the air and with her eyes burning with fire, "It cost much." Then she would take a long breath and say, "But it's worth the cost." Beloved, the anointing will cost you everything, but it's worth the cost.

Dr. Michelle Corral

Prayer

Lord, I give You honor and glory! Thank you for everything that You have done for me. I declare and decree that I will come back after every crisis. I thank You that You are using my pain to train me for greatness, and that these dark days will be used for my destiny. I thank You for Your anointing, which guarantees me preservation through every tribulation. In the mighty, victorious name of Jesus, amen!

Dr. Michelle Corral

Diary for Destiny

1. Think of a time in your life when you were able to come back after a crisis. How did the Lord arrange the circumstances of your life to enable you to come back? How did the Lord use your pain to train you for greatness?

_____

_____

_____

_____

_____

_____

2. Is there a crisis happening in your life right now? What reassurances and evidences is God currently giving you that you will come back after this crisis?

_____

_____

_____

_____

_____

Chapter Five

Yeshua Code

~The Blood Bought Guarantee for The Recovery of Your Ruins~

What is a "Bible code"? For some of us, the phrase "Bible code" causes caution and controversy. Years ago, there was a popular fad that attracted and fascinated the curiosities of believers and non-believers alike. This fad was based on the variation of Bible codes. It was a trend that instigated the studies of sequences and patterns hidden in the Bible. Some of these "codes" unveiled meanings and messages that were "secret" in nature.

This trend raises eyebrows because the discovery of secrets was not for the sake of substantiating Scripture and confirming its infallibility, but these codes only emphasized new "secrets" unveiled in the Bible.

Such Bible codes can be dangerous. The danger lies in the underlying purpose of why discovery of these codes was made. If our research leads us only to possess some "secret" knowledge outside of the parameters of Scripture, then we are entering dangerous territory.

If we are laboring in study and prayer for the sake of using the truth as a confirmation and verification of what is already written, then we will discover the true "hidden meaning" of those texts. The Bible says, "In the mouth of two or three witnesses let every word of God be established."

Deuteronomy 9:15 KJV
One witness shall not rise up against a man for any iniquity, or for any sin, in any sin that he sinneth: at the mouth of two witnesses, or at the mouth of three witnesses, shall the matter be established.

2 Corinthians 13:1 KJV
In the mouth of two or three witnesses shall every word be established.

Beloved, I believe that true "Bible codes" will serve as a witness to confirm and reaffirm what is already written. A true Bible code, like the one inscribed in the Book of Esther by Queen Esther herself in Esther 10, will confirm the infallibility and inerrancy of Scripture.

In a literal sense of Scripture, Bible codes serve as a literary device placed in the text to communicate concepts and messages that can only be extracted through proper investigation that leads to a revelation of the text. In my opinion, there are different types of Bible codes. The code that I will present to you is simple, apparent, non-ambiguous and deliberate. My intention in cracking the code in Isaiah is not to use mathematical patterns that only a theological genius could decipher. Instead, my objective is to prove to you that God has given His guarantee that the rebuilding of your ruins is already paid for. The rebuilding of your ruins is so precious to God that the "Yeshua code" will produce the proof that it is bought by the blood.

In the book of Isaiah in Chapter 40 through Chapter 66, we see prophetic announcements that are continually consistent. The nature of these prophetic announcements are specifically to Zion concerning the mercy, compassion, favor, healing, deliverance, increase, prosperity, renovation, return and recovery of her ruins. These prophetic announcements to Zion occur as God's holy protection plan during two periods of Zion's history. These prophecies of consolation and compensation serve as a protection plan that surrounds the city during a time of great vulnerability.

The first period of time that these prophetic announcements impacted was during the time that Isaiah's prophecies were initially spoken, when all the areas in the northern kingdom of Israel were vanquished by the Assyrians. The power of these prophecies served as God's protection plan against the invasion. It was the power of the spoken prophetic word through Isaiah that miraculously brought God's protective power over the city. In every surrounding city and nation, Sennacherib's war machine was devouring and destroying everything that it marched through. Yet the holy city of Jerusalem, with her walls that were so precious to God, withstood the violent standoff because of Isaiah's words continually going forth for Zion.

In the same way, you also will be able to withstand every bombardment against your destiny just like the holy city if you have the power of the prophetic word in your midst. In Scripture, we see how the power of the prophetic word caused the city to be stabilized when the city was being traumatized.

Isaiah 36:1-2 KJV
[1] Now it came to pass in the fourteenth year of king Hezekiah, that Sennacherib king of Assyria came up against

all the defenced cities of Judah, and took them. [2] And the king of Assyria sent Rabshakeh from Lachish to Jerusalem unto king Hezekiah with a great army.

Isaiah 36:4-5 KJV
[4] And Rabshakeh said unto them, Say ye now to Hezekiah, Thus saith the great king, the king of Assyria, What confidence is this wherein thou trustest? [5] I say, sayest thou, (but they are but vain words) I have counsel and strength for war: now on whom dost thou trust, that thou rebellest against me?

Notice, beloved, the words that were being spoken against Jerusalem by Rabshakeh. The text goes out of its way to teach that the siege set against Jerusalem was a spiritual siege, in which the warfare of wicked words and the overpowering army of the Assyrians were set against Jerusalem.

In Isaiah 37:21-29, the text teaches how the king of Judah fled to Isaiah the prophet for words of instruction in the midst of impending destruction. These words served as the strength of the city during the crisis. Beloved, I pray that just as the power of the prophetic word stopped the siege against Jerusalem, that you would experience the same as you embrace the power of the prophetic word written in this book.

Dr. Michelle Corral

The second period that these prophetic announcements affected is the set time of *Shivat Zion*. These prophecies were spoken approximately 164 years before the destruction of Zion by the Babylonians, showing that God was providing His divine protection plan for Jerusalem in advance. Every one of the prophetic announcements concerning the rebuilding of her ruins was made as a declaration before the devastation. This is how God's protection plan works in our lives. He's already got our back before the attack. God has already planned your deliverance before your dilemma.

These words spoken by Isaiah are words that God speaks to you right now in the areas of your desolate dreams. He says to you as He says to Zion in Isaiah 40:

Isaiah 40:1-2 KJV
[1] Comfort ye, comfort ye my people, saith your God. [2] Speak ye comfortably to Jerusalem, and cry unto her, that her warfare is accomplished.

Isaiah 49:14-16 KJV
[14] But Zion said, The Lord hath forsaken me, and my Lord hath forgotten me. [15] Can a woman forget her sucking child, that she should not have compassion on the son of her womb? yea, they may forget, yet will I not forget thee. [16] Behold, I have graven thee upon the palms of my hands; thy walls are continually before me.

A "Nothing But God" Anointing

Isaiah, Jeremiah, and other prophets primarily prophesied about *Shivat Zion*, or the return to Zion. These prophets prophesied that after the Babylonian captivity, the destruction of the Temple, and the complete annihilation of the city of Jerusalem, the Jews would return to Zion and rebuild the ruins. In the natural, it seemed impossible for millions of people to return to the land, rebuild the Temple and the city of Zion, and take back the territory. There was no hope, no human way to do that, especially without a leader. We need to understand that *Shivat Zion* and breaking out of the Babylonian captivity was completely different than the ending of the exile in Egypt. The exile in Egypt came to an end with a leader, Moses, who performed signs and wonders. Moses placed Pharaoh under subjection to the Spirit through those miracles, and led the children of Israel to the borders of the Promised Land.

But in *Shivat Zion*, we don't have a Moses figure, and we don't have miracles that we can visibly see. We don't have someone parting the Red Sea, and we don't have someone like Joshua commanding the sun to stand still so that the war might be won. God's people were divided in their commitment to return to Zion and rebuild the ruins. At least in the time of the Exodus, the people of Israel were united about their desire to leave Egypt, to get out from the burden of Pharaoh and to come into the Promised Land. But during the time of *Shivat Zion*, national unity was compromised as many remained content in their captivity. Multitudes who been given the call to return to Zion after the completion of 70 years in captivity refused to return. There were only 42,000 people who had said yes to God and had already returned to Israel, while 6 million Israelites had stayed in Babylon. So we need to understand that it was a miracle that the people of Israel returned to Zion to rebuild the ruins when they didn't have a leader like Moses, visible signs and wonders, strength, or a united vision. All they had was a Word.

There are many of us who are getting ready to rebuild the ruins in our lives. We may not have a strong leader figure to help direct us into our destiny. We may not have any finances that would enable us to have the hope and vision to believe that what the enemy stole, God will give us back. But we are in a supernatural season called "nothing but God!" Beloved, I want you to keep saying over and over, "I receive a nothing-but-God anointing and I know that I shall recover these ruins."

Dr. Michelle Corral

The Yeshua Code: Your Blood Bought Guarantee

Beloved, you may ask the question, "How do I know that I will receive the miracle of rebuilt ruins and destiny?" God's guarantee is in the blood. Your restoration after devastation miracle is already bought by the blood. Let's take a look at the book of Isaiah, Chapter 40 through Chapter 66. Why is the Yeshua code so prominent in these chapters? As a prophet to Zion, Isaiah is going to unveil God's guarantee through a code I call the Yeshua code. This code reveals to us an atonement that will be made to pay the price of ending the captivity of Zion and rebuilding her ruins. Isaiah understood that the promises of rebuilding the ruins and reoccupying the Land, and the promises of divine consolation, divine compensation, and regaining reputation, could not be earned by the people's merit. Isaiah presents an atonement offered up by a man that appears in the midst of the promises of consolation and restoration of Zion. In a theological sense of Scripture, there is a systematic engineering in the text that creates a consistent pattern with atonement.

These texts are engineered by the prophet Isaiah as a literary device that continues to appear systematically throughout the proclamation of restoration given in Chapter 40 through Chapter 66 all throughout the text. These texts are very non-ambiguous and blatantly appear

Dr. Michelle Corral

because they are inconsistent and appear to be incompatible with the messages being announced. These texts appear out of nowhere. They do not connect with the continuity of the message. They are placed there very plainly. They are used by Isaiah as this unique literary device that gives a message within the message. It is the message of atonement, a suffering servant, a man whose sacrifice is an offering of sin.

These texts are not presented only in one place but appear throughout the prophetic announcements of Zion's rebuilding of her ruins. There is no explanation about this suffering servant or why these verses are so systematic. There is no explanation about why they appear so frequently throughout the promises given to Zion's children, her ruins, her hope, her future.

In Isaiah 49:8-26, God promises restoration, divine compensation, and liberation. In Isaiah 50:6, out of nowhere appears a man offering atonement.

Isaiah 50:6 KJV
I gave my back to the smiters, and my cheeks to them that plucked off the hair: I hid not my face from shame and spitting.

In the entire chapter of Isaiah 51 and in Isaiah 52:1-12, God promises deliverance and the redemption of return. He promises the repossession of taken territory. God promises return out of the land of captivity back to Zion. He promises cancellation of their devastation. He promises a return to take possession of the promises. In Isaiah 51:10, the Israelites are called "the ransomed" and in Isaiah 51:11 they are called "the redeemed." That means they were purchased.

In Isaiah 52:13-15, the suffering servant appears as one whose visage was marred more than any other man.

Isaiah 52:13-15 KJV
[13] Behold, my servant shall deal prudently, he shall be exalted and extolled, and be very high. [14] As many were astonied at thee; his visage was so marred more than any man, and his form more than the sons of men: [15] So shall he sprinkle many nations; the kings shall shut their mouths at him: for that which had not been told them shall they see; and that which they had not heard shall they consider.

The word "sprinkle" in Isaiah 52:15 ("So shall He sprinkle many nations") is also used in Leviticus 16 for the blood of the atonement to be placed on the altar.

Leviticus 16:14 KJV
And he shall take of the blood of the bullock, and sprinkle it with his finger upon the mercy seat eastward; and before

Dr. Michelle Corral

the mercy seat shall he sprinkle of the blood with his finger seven times.

In Isaiah 53, the entire chapter is based on the atonement. The writer uses this style as a literary device in the same way that Moses inserts Genesis 38 in the book of Genesis. Have you ever wondered why everything from Genesis 37-50 is centered on Joseph, except for Genesis 38? Genesis 37 is all about Joseph, then Genesis 39-50 shows us Joseph's journey from the prison to the palace. In the midst of those chapters, Moses uses Genesis 38, the continuation of the tribe of Judah, to be a promise of atonement in the future for Israel's redemption and for Joseph's total turnaround.

Beloved, today you can claim the redemption of your ruins, the rebuilding of your waste places. You can claim the promises of taking back the territory in your life. It doesn't matter how humiliated or how devastated you may feel. It does not matter how impossible your shattered dreams may appear. God has already given His guarantee. He will redeem your dream because it is bought by the blood.

Dr. Michelle Corral

Prayer

Lord, I praise you and I give you glory! I have expectation for full restoration in my life. I give you praise right now for every promise that has been spoken into my destiny through the Word of the living God. I am redeemed by the blood of Yeshua haMashiach, Jesus the Messiah! In the name of Jesus, amen!

Dr. Michelle Corral

Diary for Destiny

1. What areas of your life need to be redeemed? What promises has God given you in His Word that He will redeem these areas of your life?

_____

_____

_____

_____

_____

2. What are you most concerned about right now? What is causing you stress or anxiety, or causing you to lose sleep? Ask the Lord to speak directly to you about these situations. What is the Lord saying to you?

_____

_____

_____

_____

_____

Dr. Michelle Corral

Chapter Six

The Power of His Promises

Beloved, I want to conclude with speaking to you about God's guarantee of rebuilding the ruins in your life. We're going to look at many scriptures that God has given us on return and recovery. God is going to pour out His anointing for you to rebuild the ruins in your life. When we look at the book of Jeremiah, we see that Jeremiah prophesied the destruction that was going to happen to Israel, but no one heard his words. But before the destruction and devastation actually took place, Jeremiah also prophesied consolation. These words of consolation were so strong that I believe right now, right where you are, these words of consolation are coming into you.

Jeremiah 29:10 KJV
For thus saith the LORD, That after seventy years be accomplished at Babylon I will visit you, and perform my good word toward you, in causing you to return to this place.

God has a good word toward you. It's a word of prosperity and it's a word of return and recovery. The Lord said, "After seventy years ... I will perform my good word toward you." Seventy is an atonement number. We need to understand that everything in

MC+
God has a good word toward you. It's a word of prosperity and it's a word of return and recovery.

during this Tisha B'Av period and everything related to *Shivat Tzion* or the return to Zion is in symbols that are related to the atonement. Seventy is an atonement number, 10 times 7. Anytime we see 10 and 7, or a combination of those numbers, we are talking about atonement, as we see in Leviticus 23.

Leviticus 23:27 KJV
Also on the tenth day of this seventh month there shall be a day of atonement: it shall be an holy convocation unto you; and ye shall afflict your souls, and offer an offering made by fire unto the LORD.

Atonement is a prophetic prefiguring of the blood of Jesus, so we understand that what we are about to receive on Tisha B'Av has already been bought by the blood of Jesus. Seventy years is a symbol of atonement. It is a symbol of atonement covering you and me. We cannot and do not have to depend on our own righteousness or our own strength, and we understand that God is going to rebuild the ruins based on the blood of Jesus.

We see another promise of restoration in the book of Jeremiah when we read about the prophet Jeremiah and his relative Hanameel. In Jeremiah 32, we see that Jeremiah has been put into prison once again, as happened multiple times during his lifetime. This time, God tells him to do something that doesn't make much sense. Jeremiah 32:7 says, "Behold, Hanameel the son of Shallum thine uncle shall come unto thee saying, Buy thee my field that is in Anathoth: for the right of redemption is thine to buy it."

Remember that Anathoth was a Levitical city or strip of land where the priests lived. Moses and Joshua had allocated the land of Israel to the tribes and their families, and God didn't ever want any of those territories and lands to be taken out of the hands of the families. This is why the Lord said to Jeremiah, "Your relative is going to come and he's going to offer you a piece of land to redeem." Scripture continues:

Dr. Michelle Corral

Jeremiah 32:8-9 KJV
[8] So Hanameel mine uncle's son came to me in the court
of the prison according to the word of the Lord, and said
unto me, Buy my field, I pray thee, that is in Anathoth,
which is in the country of Benjamin: for the right of
inheritance is thine, and the redemption is thine; buy it for
thyself. Then I knew that this was the word of the Lord. [9]
And I bought the field of Hanameel my uncle's son, that
was in Anathoth, and weighed him the money, even
seventeen shekels of silver.

Seventeen is also a supernatural symbol of atonement. Remember that whenever we see 10 and 7, or a combination of 10 and 7 (e.g., 10 plus 7, 10 times 7), we see a prophetic parallel of the atonement and a prophetic prefiguring of the work of the blood of Jesus. The day of atonement, on the tenth day of the seventh Biblical month, was a day every year when everything became reconciled. And every 50 years on the day of atonement during the year of jubilee, every man returned back to his land and every piece of property had to return to its original owner. So we need to understand that ten and seven are symbols of the blood and the work of the atonement in our lives.

We also need to understand that the silver represents the silver that the Son of God was sold for. Matthew 26:15 tells us that Yeshua was sold for silver, which is a prophetic prefiguring of the atonement of souls: "And said unto them, what will ye give me, and I will deliver Him unto you? And they covenanted with him for thirty pieces of silver."

So we see that the prophet Jeremiah is going to purchase his relative Hanameel's piece of property for 17 shekels of silver. Let's continue with our study of Scripture:

Jeremiah 32:11-15 KJV
[11] So I took the evidence of the purchase, both that which was sealed according to the law and custom, and that which was open: [12] And I gave the evidence of the purchase unto Baruch the son of Neriah, the son of Maaseiah, in the sight of Hanameel mine uncle's son, and in the presence of the witnesses that subscribed the book of the purchase, before all the Jews that sat in the court of the prison. [13] And I charged Baruch before them, saying, [14] Thus saith the Lord of hosts, the God of Israel; Take these evidences, this evidence of the purchase, both which is sealed, and this evidence which is open; and put them in an earthen vessel, that they may continue many days. [15] For thus saith the Lord of hosts, the God of Israel; Houses and fields and vineyards shall be possessed again in this land.

When Jeremiah purchased the piece of property with 17 pieces of silver, God was giving the children of Israel a guarantee that when they were taken out of the land of

Dr. Michelle Corral

Israel, they would come back and repossess the land. God was promising the children of Israel that when they were taken to Babylon, when they seemed to have been distanced from their destiny and had lost everything, that they were going to get it all back. God is saying the same thing to us - we have blood evidence that we are going to take back the territory! All we need to do is believe what God has written in His Word.

We see further promises that the Lord brings about restoration and recovery in Jeremiah 30.

Jeremiah 30:3 KJV
For, lo, the days come, saith the LORD, that I will bring again the captivity of my people Israel and Judah, saith the LORD: and I will cause them to return to the land that I gave to their fathers, and they shall possess it.

When Jerusalem was destroyed, the people were taken out of their land and they were brought to a place that looked like they would never be able to return. Some of you have been brought to a place where you've said, "I'll never be able to return to what I had before. I'll never be able to get out of this place of depression or this place of desolation. I am stuck in this place and I can't get out. I'm in bondage." But I am here today to tell you that the anointing of Tisha B'Av is lifting you up out of where you are and bringing you into the promise of God. You're going to break out of this place for the glory of God and return to who you are supposed to be!

Sometimes when we are in a trial and we're going through suffering, the first thing that happens is an identity crisis. We begin to lose our identity, and we begin to relate more to our circumstances than to who we actually are. Some of us have been going through great personal pain. We've been going through pain, rejection, and hurts for so many years that we have now actually identified so strongly with the desolation that it feels as if our name has been changed and our identity has been changed. We no longer identify with the promises of God. We no longer identify with the days when God was bringing success and when God was opening doors for us. We now have an identity that's based on sorrow, suffering, disappointment, and pain. But I am here to tell you that the identity thief is about to return your identity, and you're about to get your identity back! That's what these verses in Jeremiah are all about. You're going back to who you're supposed to be and back to your true self!

MC+

I am here to tell you that the identity thief is about to return your identity, and you're about to get your identity back!

Jeremiah 30:10 KJV
Therefore fear thou not, O my servant Jacob, saith the LORD; neither be dismayed, O Israel: for, lo, I will save thee from afar, and thy seed from the land of their captivity; and Jacob shall return, and shall be in rest, and be quiet, and none shall make him afraid.

Jeremiah is talking about an identity of being in a dark place, an identity of not possessing the promises of God, an identity of being in a place distanced from your destiny where you can't see anything happening in your life and where there is no hope. You need to know that God has already said through Jeremiah the prophet, "I'm going to cause you to return. I will save you from afar and you shall return."

Jeremiah 31:8 KJV
Behold, I will bring them from the north country, and gather them from the coasts of the earth, and with them the blind and the lame, the woman with child and her that travaileth with child together: a great company shall return thither.

Jeremiah 32:44 KJV
Men shall buy fields for money, and subscribe evidences, and seal them, and take witnesses in the land of Benjamin, and in the places about Jerusalem, and in the cities of Judah, and in the cities of the mountains, and in the cities

of the valley, and in the cities of the south: for I will cause their captivity to return, saith the LORD.

Jeremiah 33:11 KJV
The voice of joy, and the voice of gladness, the voice of the bridegroom, and the voice of the bride, the voice of them that shall say, Praise the LORD of hosts: for the LORD is good; for his mercy endureth for ever: and of them that shall bring the sacrifice of praise into the house of the LORD. For I will cause to return the captivity of the land, as at the first, saith the LORD.

Jeremiah 33:26 KJV
Then will I cast away the seed of Jacob and David my servant, so that I will not take any of his seed to be rulers over the seed of Abraham, Isaac, and Jacob: for I will cause their captivity to return, and have mercy on them.

Continue to declare this until your victory has been won: "In the name of Jesus, the God that I serve is bringing me back to where I used to be. The latter part is going to be greater than the former. I'm taking back territory. God is bringing me back to my true self. God is bringing me back to the place of hope. God is bringing me back to the place of vision!"

We've seen throughout these texts the word "return" being used, which comes from the Hebrew root *shub*

(Strong's Hebrew 7725). From an English language perspective, it seems that the Lord is saying, "I will cause these people to return to this place. I will cause them to return to the land." But we need to understand that "return" in Hebrew also means "recover." So we could also read this verse as saying, "I'm going to cause a great company to recover. I'm going to cause a great company to come back and recover the land."

The Hebrew root *shub* can also be translated as "restore." In fact, *shub* is translated as "restore" hundreds of times in the Hebrew Scriptures. So that means that God is going to cause you to be restored. God is going to cause everything to be restored back to your life!

We need to understand that the Hebrew word for return not only means to recover, it not only means to restore, but it also means to reverse! God is going to reverse some things! Some things in your life are about to be reversed from the way the devil has wanted it; things are going to turn around! There's going to be *vena haphak* (from Strong's Hebrew 2015), a divine turnaround. Things are going to turn around 360 degrees. Return means to reverse!

Jeremiah 33:14 KJV
Behold, the days come, saith the LORD, that I will perform that good thing which I have promised unto the house of

Israel and to the house of Judah.

The good thing that God has promised to your vision, your dream, your destiny, your future, He's going to cause to happen even today on Tisha B'Av! Beloved people, what is so important to the spark of a soul that has been ignited by Torah? There is hope for you. You are not forgotten by God. He wants you to know that you will experience a personal *Shivat Zion* because this is the season of your divine turnaround.

Psalm 16:9 KJV
Therefore my heart is glad, and my glory rejoiceth: my flesh also shall rest in hope.

Psalm 31:24 KJV
Be of good courage, and he shall strengthen your heart, all ye that hope in the LORD.

Today you don't have to be filled with anxiety because God has given you hope.

Psalm 33:18 KJV
Behold, the eye of the LORD is upon them that fear him, upon them that hope (tikvah) in his mercy (rachem).

Psalm 33:2 KJV
Let thy mercy, O LORD, be upon us, according as we hope in

thee.

Psalm 71:5 KJV
For thou art my hope, O Lord GOD: thou art my trust from my youth.

Today I want you to receive hope again to know that this is not the end. When you saw your dream burnt to the ground, that is not who you are. When you saw your dream go up in smoke and you ended up at ground zero and you cried so many tears that you couldn't even cry anymore, you need to know that God is saying *tikvah*! Today on Tisha B'Av you are going to regain your dream! God is going to rebuild your dream again!

Jeremiah 31:17 KJV
And there is hope in thine end, saith the LORD, that thy children shall come again to their own border.

Acts 2:26 KJV
Therefore did my heart rejoice, and my tongue was glad; moreover also my flesh shall rest in hope.

Romans 5:5 KJV
And hope maketh not ashamed; because the love of God is shed abroad in our hearts by the Holy Ghost which is given unto us.

If we are hoping, then we are not going to be ashamed because God is faithful to perform His promises to us! The Bible says that through hope and patience, we will possess the promises (Hebrews 6:12). I want you to know that God has given you hope, and I want you to understand that this is a season of rebuilding ruins.

Beloved, let me remind you again that God's nature as revealed in His Word is to show you that before you ever went through a crisis, before you ever went through your trial and your tribulation, before you ever saw your dream torched to flames, God had already prophesied your return and your recovery. That's the whole supernatural secret of the book of Isaiah. One hundred and fifty four years before Zion burnt to the ground, God was already prophesying return and recovery, He was already prophesying consolation and restoration before the city ever burnt, before anybody ever invaded the city. Right now, God is already speaking comeback to you. God is already speaking return. God is already speaking recovery. God is saying, "I'm more concerned about your comeback than the crisis that you're in!"

MC+

God is saying, "I'm more concerned about your comeback than the crisis that you're in!"

Some of us are so upset, so hurt, so broken, so stuck in a crisis that we think it's up to us to plan our comeback. But we serve a God who is an expert at coming back. He's already got everything new prepared for you. He's already got your new ministry, your new calling, your new place, your new clothes, your new friends, and your new relationships, and your comeback is going to be much greater than your crisis ever was. You need to understand that you serve a God who is an expert on bringing you back!

MC+
You need to understand that you serve a God who is an expert on bringing you back!

You may be weeping and saying, "God, I don't understand why I'm going through this!" But I'm here to tell you that there is hope, there is purpose to your pain, and there is purpose to your trial. God is pouring out His anointing this season to rebuild the ruins in your life as He promised in His word. God's promises are good and true, and we can surely hope in the Lord, *HaTikvah*!

Prayer

Lord, I thank You that You are my hope and salvation! I thank You that You are a God who brings return, recovery, and restoration. I praise You that no matter what things look like, You already have a comeback plan for me! In the name of Jesus, amen!

Dr. Michelle Corral

Diary for Destiny

1. Where are you seeing return, restoration, and recovery happen in your life? Remember that this is your time of divine turnaround and personal *Shivat Zion*!

_____

_____

_____

_____

_____

2. How has your hope been renewed by reading this book? What verses of Scripture will you stand on to maintain and increase your hope in the days ahead as the Lord continues to be the Rebuilder of Your Ruins?

_____

_____

_____

_____

_____

Chesed Publishing

What is Chesed?

Chesed means "loving kindness" in Hebrew. Our publication house is called Chesed Publishing because when you purchase a book, you are helping us to do the impossible for people that could never help themselves.

We provide daily feeding programs to orphans and grandmothers, pay for educational fees for children in our orphan homes, conduct medical missions throughout the world, purchase clean water wells, and so much more.

In April 2016, Chesed Publishing was founded to financially support Dr. Michelle Corral's vision of acts of chesed to the poor, along with the mission to pass on the wealth of teaching that God entrusted to her to the next generation.

Books Authored by Dr. Michelle Corral

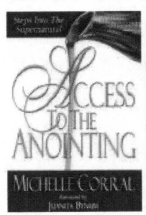

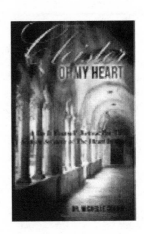

Dr. Michelle Corral

For a Complete List of
CDs and Ministry Resources

Contact:

Breath of the Spirit Prophetic Word Center
P.O. BOX 2676
Orange, CA 92859

Phone # (714) 694-1100

Youtube.com/DrMichelleCorral
Word Network on Mondays
@ 10:30 pm PST
www.breathofthespirit.org
www.drmichellecorral.com
facebook.com/Dr.Corral

Made in the USA
San Bernardino, CA
22 September 2018